Oh, no... it's **The Moe & Joe Show!** ®   **Moe:** Say, Joe! What do flies read? **Joe:** Well, Moe... The Mighty Bug Book of Riddles!

MIGHTY BIG HA! BOOK OF RIDDLES

LIBRARY O' LAUGHS

DEDICATED to
CASTRELLA
YOU RULE!

LIBRARY OF CONGRESS CONTROL NUMBER : 2001091222

ISBN 0-8431-7583-4
B C D E F G H I J

PSS! IS A REGISTERED TRADEMARK OF PENGUIN PUTNAM BOOKS FOR YOUNG READERS,
NEW YORK
THE MOE & JOE SHOW AND MAD ADDS ARE TRADEMARKS OF CRAIG YOE STUDIO, INC.
MOE & JOE © 2001 CRAIG YOE STUDIO, INC.

MIGHTY BIG BOOK OF RIDDLES

HA!

by CRAIG YOE

WEBMASTER OF
WWW.RIDDLES4KIDS.COM

LIBRARY O LAUGHS

PSS!
PRICE STERN SLOAN
NEW YORK

THIS BOOK IS MANY PEOPLE'S BABY. FIRST A *BIG THANKS* TO *CLIZIA GUSSONI, JON ANDERSON, JAYNE ANTIPOW, PATRICIA PASQUALE,* AND *REBECCA GOLDBERG,* WHOSE WORK WAS ESSENTIAL TO THE SUCCESS OF THIS BOOK. IT INCLUDED NUMBERLESS ROUNDS OF PROOF READING, SLEEPLESS NIGHTS, QUALITY CONTROL, COORDINATION, MANAGEMENT, WRITING AND RE-WRITING.

WE WOULD ALSO LIKE TO *THANK* THE FOLLOWING PEOPLE FOR THEIR HARD WORK: *TRACEY ARMISTO-VITOLO, CINDY BARRY, JOY COURT, DARREN CRUZ, JODI HUELIN, ROSALIE LENT, PAULA MAESTRO-SALAT, MIKE MARRO, LUKE McDONNELL, ANGELA NAPOSKI, KRIS REINHOLD, ARTHUR SCHOEDEL, BETTY SOKOL, SCOTT SMITH, PAUL STONE, AVARELLE, VALISSA, DONOVAN, CARLOS,* AND ESPECIALLY *MOE & JOE,* WHO TOOK TIME FROM THEIR BUSY SCHEDULES TO APPEAR IN THESE PAGES!

@ MAD ADD JOKE!

$$\frac{\text{AQUARIUMS} + \text{GRATITUDE}}{\text{FISH THANKS}}$$

WHEN I WAS A *WEE LAD* MY *DAD'S FRIEND* ENCOURAGED ME TO START A *NOTEBOOK OF RIDDLES.* WELL, IT'S FINISHED NOW – WHAT DO YOU *THINK?*

I WAS ONCE THRILLED TO MEET AND INTERVIEW *BOB DUNN,* THE GUY WHO INVENTED THE *KNOCK-KNOCK JOKE.* I'M AN INVENTOR NOW *MYSELF* AND WANTED TO INVENT MY *OWN* JOKE. SO, YOU'LL FIND HERE IN THE FOLLOWING PAGES... *MAD ADDS®!* WHAT DO YOU *THINK?*

FOR *MORE* RIDDLES, VISIT *RIDDLES4KIDS.COM* AND YOU CAN GIVE US SOME OF *YOUR OWN* JOKES FOR OUR *NEXT* BOOK!

YOUR PAL,

CRAIG

CRAIG YOE.

YOE!

WHAT'S WORSE THAN *FINDING* A *WORM* IN AN *APPLE*?

Yoe!

... FINDING *HALF* A WORM!

HY DO *SCIENTISTS* LOOK FOR THINGS *OVER AND OVER*?

... BECAUSE THEY *RE*-SEARCH EVERYTHING!

$$\frac{\text{CASPER} + \text{CORN FLAKES}}{\text{GHOST TOASTIES}}$$

WHY DID THE **DOG** RUN **AWAY**
FROM **HOME?**

... **DOG-GONE** IF I KNOW!

WHAT KIND OF **SOUP** DO **DOGS** LIKE?

 ... CHICKEN **POODLE!**

HAT HAPPENED TO THE **DOG** THAT
SWALLOWED THE **WATCH?**

... HE GOT LOTS OF **TICKS!**

WHAT IS AN *ALIEN DOCTOR'S* FAVORITE *TV SHOW?*

... THE *"X-RAY FILES!"*

 HY DIDN'T THE *SKELETON* CROSS THE *ROAD?*

... BECAUSE HE DIDN'T HAVE THE *GUTS!*

 a MAD ADD JOKE!

ORANGE BEAR
+ A GHOST
———————
WINNIE THE BOO

Oh, no... it's **The Moe & Joe Show!** ® *Moe*: Say, Joe! Where was the Declaration of Independence signed?

Joe: Well, Moe... at the bottom!

HAT IS ALWAYS *BROKEN* BEFORE
IT IS *EATEN?*

... AN *EGG!*

WHEN WILL A *BLACK DOG* USUALLY ENTER
A *RED HOUSE?*

... WHEN THE *DOOR IS OPEN!*

WHY DID THE **DUCK** WEAR A **NOSE RING?**

... BECAUSE IT **FIT THE BILL!**

WHY DID THE **CHICKEN** GET **GROUNDED?**

 ... HE WAS USING **FOWL LANGUAGE!**

SKUNK
+ KANGAROO
――――――――
STINK-A-ROO

WHY WERE YOU *JUMPING UP AND DOWN?*

... I JUST TOOK MY *MEDICINE* AND FORGOT TO *SHAKE THE BOTTLE!*

WHAT DID THE *COMPOSER* DO TO IMPROVE HIS *TENNIS GAME?*

... HE WORKED ON HIS *BACH*-STROKE!

WHAT'S THE DIFFERENCE BETWEEN A *SHINY DIME* AND A *DIRTY QUARTER?*

... 15 CENTS!

WHAT DOES A *KID* WATCH WHEN HE IS *ILL?*

... *SICK*-ELODEON!

WHAT *SONG* MAKES YOU *LAUGH?*

... "*TICKLE TICKLE LITTLE STAR!*"

WHY DOES *JAY LENO* RIDE A *MOTORCYCLE?*

... HE SAW A SIGN THAT SAID "*NO JAY WALKING!*"

Oh, no... it's **The Moe & Joe Show!** ®   **Moe**: Say, Joe! What building is low in calories?

 Joe: Well, Moe... a lighthouse!

WHY CAN'T YOUR *HEAD* BE *12 INCHES LONG?*

... BECAUSE THEN IT WOULD BE A *FOOT!*

@ MAD ADD JOKE!

A CRIMINAL + A PIECE OF BREAD / AMERICA'S TOAST WANTED

WHY DID THE *SWIMMER* CALL HIS *BARBER* BEFORE THE *BIG RACE?*

... TO *SHAVE* A *COUPLE OF SECONDS* OFF HIS *TIME!*

HOW DO *YOU* STOP A *SCARF* FROM SLIPPING DOWN A *GIRAFFE'S NECK?*

... TIE A *KNOT* IN HIS *NECK!*

HOW DOES A *TOAD* END HIS *E-MAILS?*

... *"HOP TO SEE YOU SOON!"*

A SHEEP
+ CAPED CRUSADER
―――――――――
BAA-ATMAN

WHAT DOES A *SQUIRREL* LIKE TO *WATCH* ON *TV?*
... CARTOON *NUT*-WORK!

WHY DID THE *COW* CROSS THE *ROAD?*

... TO GET TO THE *UDDER* SIDE!

HAT *FRUIT* IS *YELLOW AND BLUE?*

... AN *UNHAPPY BANANA!*

 Oh, no... it's **The Moe & Joe Show!** ® **Moe**: Say, Joe! What bird can lift the most weight?

Joe: Well, Moe... a crane!

 HAT *STARTS* WITH A *"T"*, IS FILLED WITH *"T"*, AND *ENDS* WITH A *"T"*?

... A *TEAPOT!*

WHICH OF *NOAH'S ANIMALS* DIDN'T COME IN *PAIRS?*

... THE *WORMS*...THEY CAME IN *APPLES!*

Oh, no... it's **The Moe & Joe Show!** ® *Moe*: Say, Joe! What kind of cereal do you get in bed?

 Joe: Well, Moe... Bed Post Toasties!

DID YOU **HEAR** THE ONE ABOUT THE **CROW** WHO **SAT** ON THE **TELEPHONE POLE?**

BLAH! BLAH! BLAH!

... HE WANTED TO MAKE A **LONG DISTANCE CAW!**

WHAT WOULD **OLD MACDONALD** SAY IF HE WERE A **RAPPER?**

... "E-I-E-I-**YO!**"

@ **MAD ADD** JOKE!

AGENT 007
+ MADONNA
_____
JAMES BLONDE

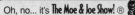 Oh, no... it's **The Moe & Joe Show!** ® *Moe*: Say, Joe! What's the best thing to put in a hot dog?

 Joe: Well, Moe... your teeth!

WHERE DOES YOUR *MOM* KEEP HER *CAR?*

... THE DEPARTMENT OF *MOTHER* VEHICLES!

 HY DOES *DRACULA* LOVE *COMPUTERS?*

... BECAUSE OF THE *MEGA-BITES!*

HOW MANY *FEET* ARE IN A *YARD?*

 ...THAT DEPENDS ON HOW MANY *PEOPLE* ARE *STANDING IN IT!*

WHICH *PET STORE PRODUCT* MAKES A *CAT* GO TO *SLEEP?*

... *CAT-NAP!*

WHEN DID THE *CHICKEN* CROSS THE *ROAD?*

... AT *EGGS*-ACTLY THE RIGHT TIME!

GIRAFFES
+ DISNEY WORLD
——————————
NECKS IN LINE!

WHERE DOES *TONY THE TIGER* PLAY *FOOTBALL?*

... IN THE *CEREAL BOWL!*

HAT KIND OF *INSECT* DO YOU *SWALLOW* TO RELIEVE A *COLD?*

... A DECONGEST-*ANT!*

WHAT FAMOUS *ENGLISH WRITER*
WRITES *ROCK SONGS?*

... *SHAKE,* RATTLE & ROLL-*SPEAR!*

WHAT IS *MOTHER GOOSE'S*
FAVORITE *PASTA?*

... MACARONI AND *GEESE!*

Oh, no... it's **The Moe & Joe Show!** ® *Moe*: Say, Joe! Did you hear the one about the sick dog?

Joe: Well, Moe... his barf was worse than his bite!

WHAT IS AT THE *END* OF THE *ROAD?*

... THE LETTER *"D"!*

HAT CAN *SPEAK* EVERY *LANGUAGE* BUT NEVER *WENT TO SCHOOL?*

... *AN ECHO!*

WHAT SHOULD *YOU* KNOW BEFORE TEACHING A *DOG* NEW *TRICKS?*

... *MORE* THAN THE *DOG!*

 A GHOST + A FAMOUS PAINTING
——————————————
THE MOAN-A LISA

WHAT'S A **BEE'S** FAVORITE **HAIRCUT?**

   ... A **BUZZ** CUT!

HAT KIND OF **FRUIT** DID **NOAH** TAKE ON THE **ARK?**

... **PEARS!**

Oh, no... it's **The Moe & Joe Show!** ® *Moe*: Say, Joe! How do you make a green monster?

 Joe: Well, Moe... cross a yellow monster with a blue one!

WHY DID THE **BEE** GET SENT TO THE **PRINCIPAL'S OFFICE?**

... BECAUSE OF HIS BAD BEE-*HIVE*-IOR!

WHICH **NOTE** DOES A **BUZZING INSECT** PLAY?

... **BEE**-SHARP!

TARZAN
+ A GREAT PRESIDENT
―――――――――――――
APE LINCOLN

BERRY FUNNY

DEPARTMENT

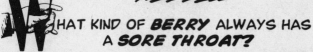

WHAT KIND OF *BERRY* ALWAYS HAS A *SORE THROAT?*

... A *RASP*-BERRY!

WHAT KIND OF *BERRY* ALWAYS SEEMS *SAD?*

... A *BLUE*-BERRY!

WHAT KIND OF *BERRY* MAKES A *LOUD, HONKING SOUND?*

... A *GOOSE*-BERRY!

WHAT KIND OF *BERRY* NEEDS HELP *DRINKING* FROM A *GLASS?*

... A *STRAW*-BERRY!

WHAT *BERRIES* DO *GIRLS* LIKE?

... *BOYS*-ENBERRIES!

A HULA HOOP
+ A 2-DOOR SPORTS CAR
A HULA-COUPE

WHAT DID THE *BOY SNAKE* GIVE TO THE *GIRL SNAKE* AT THE END OF THEIR *DATE*?

... A GOOD NIGHT *HISS!*

WHAT DID THE *MOTHER TURTLE* SAY TO THE *SHY BABY TURTLE*?

... "YOU SHOULD COME OUT OF YOUR *SHELL!*"

IN WHAT **PART** OF THE **FOREST** IS
THE **FOOD STORED?**

... THE **PAN-TREE!**

WHAT DO **YOU** CALL A
HAMBURGER'S COMPLAINT?

... **GROUND BEEF!**

@ **MAD ADD JOKE!**

A RED-HAIRED GIRL
+ AN APPLE FARM
_____
LITTLE ORCHARD ANNIE

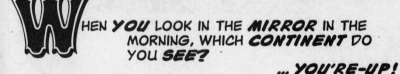

THREE NERDS WERE UNDER **ONE UMBRELLA**, BUT THEY **DIDN'T GET WET** — HOW COME?

... IT WASN'T **RAINING!**

WHAT **TOOL** DOES A **CARPENTER** NEED TO BUILD A **PLAYGROUND?**

... A **SEE-SAW!**

Oh, no... it's **The Moe & Joe Show!** ®

Moe: Say, Joe! Did you hear the one about the paratrooper?

Joe: Well, Moe... chute, no!

WHAT DOES THE **JOKE WRITER** WEAR **UNDER** HIS **PANTS?**

 ... **PUN**-DERWEAR!

WHAT KIND OF *LETTERS* DOES *DRACULA* LIKE TO *RECEIVE?*

... *FANG* MAIL!

WHAT KIND OF *TRANSPORTATION* DO *YOU* USE TO GET TO THE *BATHROOM?*

... THE *TUB*-WAY!

@ MAD ADD JOKE!

CORN ON THE COB
+ CHICKEN
―――――――――――
KERNEL SANDERS

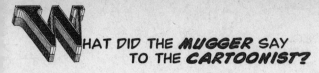

WHAT DID THE *MUGGER* SAY TO THE *CARTOONIST?*

... "YOUR *MONEY* OR YOUR *LAUGH!*"

WHAT DID THE *CHEERLEADER* SAY TO THE *SUSHI?*

... "*RAW! RAW! RAW!*"

WHY IS *DAFFY DUCK* SO *NUTTY?*

... HE'S *QUACKED* IN THE HEAD!

Oh, no... it's **The Moe & Joe Show!** ® *Moe*: Say, Joe! What's a dog's favorite melon?

 Joe: Well, Moe... a pant-elope!

WHAT DOES A *MOUNTAIN* USE
TO *PLAY BASEBALL?*

... A SUM-*MITT!*

HY DID THE *PRUNE* LOSE AT *NASCAR?*

... *DUH,* IT MADE TOO MANY *PIT* STOPS!

WHICH *U.S. PRESIDENT* BECAME A *BUTTERFLY?*

... JIMMY CARTER-*PILLAR!*

@ MAD ADD JOKE!®

AN EGG
+ A SMALL GERMAN CAR
―――――――――――――――
A YOLKS-WAGON

HOW LONG WILL YOU **LIVE** IF YOU **SMOKE CIGARETTES?**

... NOT FOR **LUNG!**

HOW DOES ONE **FROG** GREET **ANOTHER?**

... **"WART'S** UP?!"

@ **MAD ADD** JOKE!

$$\frac{ENGLAND + KERMIT}{LONDON \ FROG}$$

WHAT'S THE **DIFFERENCE** BETWEEN THE **NORTH POLE** AND THE **SOUTH POLE?**

... ALL THE DIFFERENCE IN THE **WORLD!**

WHAT IS A **RAPPER'S** FAVORITE **FOOD?**

... **YO**-GURT!

WHAT DO **BASKETBALL PLAYERS** AND **BABIES** HAVE IN **COMMON?**

 ... THEY BOTH **DRIBBLE!**

Oh, no... it's **The Moe & Joe Show!** ® *Moe*: Say, Joe! How did the caboose learn to ride a bike?

 Joe: Well, Moe... with train-ing wheels!

DO *YOU* KNOW WHAT MY *FATHER'S SISTER* LOVES ON HER *PIZZA?*

... *AUNT-* CHOVIES!

HICH *U.S. PRESIDENT* MAKES YOU THINK OF A *VACUUM CLEANER?*

 ... PRESIDENT *HOOVER!*

WHAT *BUS* CROSSED THE *ATLANTIC OCEAN?*

... THE *COLUM*-BUS!

WHAT'S A **SKUNK'S** FAVORITE **DESSERT?**

... SMELL-O!

@ **MAD ADD JOKE!**

BODY OF WATER + A WHITE BIRD
_____
A BAY-GULL

HOW DOES A **JIGSAW PUZZLE** EAT?

... PIECEMEAL!

WHAT IS MORE *UNUSUAL* THAN A *SINGING DOG?*

... A SPELLING BEE!

WHY DID *KING KONG* CLIMB UP THE *EMPIRE STATE BUILDING?*

... THE ELEVATOR WAS *OUT OF ORDER!*

@ MAD ADD JOKE!®

DOG
+ DRAWING
─────────────
FETCH-A-SKETCH

Oh, no... it's **The Moe & Joe Show!** ® *Moe*: Say, Joe! Why did the rock star scratch his ear?

Joe: Well, Moe... that's where he itched!

WHY DID THE **MOMMA INSECT** GROUND THE **KID INSECT?**

... FOR MIS-**BEE**-HAVING!

WHAT IS THE **OPPOSITE** OF A **HAIR DRYER?**

 ... A **TOE WETTER!**

WHAT KIND OF *SHIRT* CAN YOU *DRINK?*

... A *TEA*-SHIRT!

WHAT'S *GREEN* AND A POPULAR *TV NETWORK* FOR *KIDS?*

... *PICKLE*-ODEON!

WHERE DOES A *WORM* LIKE TO *VACATION?*

... THE *BIG APPLE!*

WHAT DOES A *BURGLAR* LIKE IN HIS *SOUP?*

... A *SAFE CRACKER!*

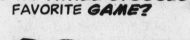HAT'S THE *THREE STOOGES'* FAVORITE *GAME?*

 ... *MOE*-NOPOLY!

@ MAD ADD JOKE!

THE THREE STOOGES + A PLACE TO STAY

LARRY, CURLY, AND MOE-TEL!

WHERE DO *YOU* TAKE A *SNAKE* THAT'S
BEEN IN AN *ACCIDENT?*

... TO THE *HISS*-PITAL!

HAT WERE *MOE* AND *JOE* BEFORE THEY
BECAME *COMEDIANS?*

 ... *HEAD*-WAITERS!

$$\frac{1,000 \text{ RAM} + \text{MOSQUITOES}}{\text{MEGA-BITES}}$$

WHAT **ROOF** IS ALWAYS **WET?**

... THE **ROOF** OF **YOUR MOUTH!**

WHAT DID THE **CEREAL** SAY TO THE **JUICE** AT BREAKFAST?

... HE PROPOSED A **TOAST!**

WHAT **SERVICE** DID **FROSTY THE SNOWMAN** ADD TO HIS **PHONE?**

... **COOL**-WAITING!

Oh, no... it's **The Moe & Joe Show!** ® *Moe*: Say, Joe! What did the scissors say to the knife?

 Joe: Well, Moe... "You look sharp!"

WHAT'S A *FARM ANIMAL'S* FAVORITE *PASTA?*

... SPA-*GOAT*-TI!

WHICH *ANIMAL* IS *NOTHING* LIKE A *HOUND DOG?*

... *EWE* AIN'T NOTHIN' LIKE A HOUND DOG!

HY WAS THE *VET* SO *BUSY?*

... BECAUSE IT WAS *RAINING CATS AND DOGS!*

WHAT DOES A *CARPENTER* DO WHEN HE *WORKS* IN THE *HOT SUN?*

Yoe!

... HE SWEATS NAILS!

WHAT DOESN'T A *POLICEMAN* LIKE ON *TOAST?*

... TRAFFIC JAM!

$$\frac{A\ COMPUTER + A\ CASHEW}{INTER\text{-}NUT}$$

WHAT'S A *CROCODILE HUNTER'S* FAVORITE THING TO *DRINK?*

... ALLI-*GATOR*-ADE!

WHAT DO *YOU* CALL IT IF YOU *BELCH* AFTER EATING A *PEAR?*

... A RE-PEAR!

@ **MAD ADD** JOKE!

A BEAR
+ A BEAUTICIAN
―――――――――
WINNIE THE SHAM-POOH

Oh, no... it's **The Moe & Joe Show!** ® *Moe*: Say, Joe! How does a storm call ahead?

 Joe: Well, Moe... on a ty-phone!

WHY DON'T *COWS* TAKE *CRUISES*?

... BECAUSE THEY GET *MOO*-TION SICKNESS!

WHAT DO *YOU* GIVE A *SHEEP* YOU BORROW *MONEY* FROM?

... AN I. O. *EWE!*

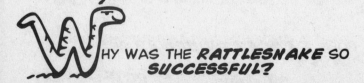

HY WAS THE *RATTLESNAKE* SO *SUCCESSFUL*?

... HE HAD A GREAT *POISON*-ALITY!

SLIMY FISH
+ KIDNEY OR LIMA
JELLY-BEANS

WHY DO **FISH** HAVE **SCALES** AND LIVE
IN THE **WATER?**

... SO YOU CAN TELL THEM APART
FROM A **BANANA!**

WHAT DOES A **NERVOUS CARPENTER** DO?

 ... BITES HIS **NAILS!**

WHY DID THE **GARBAGE CAN** GET **THROWN OUT** OF THE **HOTEL ROOM?**

... BECAUSE IT **TRASHED** THE PLACE!

Oh, no... it's **The Moe & Joe Show!** ®

Moe: Say, Joe! Did I tell you the joke about cows?

Joe: Well, Moe... I already herd it!

WHAT IS THE **LION-TAMING ACT** AT THE **CIRCUS?**

... THE **MANE** EVENT!

HERE DOES THE **ANT EATER** GO TO GET HIS **PRESCRIPTIONS FILLED?**

... TO THE **ANT FARM**-ACY!

Oh, no,.. it's **The Moe & Joe Show!** ® *Moe*: Say, Joe! What kind of party did Ernie throw for Bert?

Joe: Well, Moe... a Bert-day party!

WHERE DID THE *QUEEN BEE* GO TO *SCHOOL?*

... *BUZZ*-NESS SCHOOL!

WHAT'S A *CHICKEN'S* FAVORITE *DESSERT?*

 ... A *COOP*-CAKE!

HY DIDN'T THE *BANANA* GO TO *WORK?*

... IT HAD A *SPLITTING HEADACHE!*

WHAT DOES A *TAILOR* DO BEFORE GOING ON *VACATION?*

... HE WATERS *HIS PANTS!*

WHAT KIND OF *EXERCISE* CAN YOU DO ON A *BOAT?*

... A-*ROW*-BICS!

A PIRATE
+ A JOKER
―――――――
CAPTAIN KIDDER

@ MAD + + JOKE!

WHAT'S A *DOG'S* FAVORITE *SNACK?*

... *PUP*-CORN!

WHAT WAS THE *YOUNG DOG* VOTED IN *SCHOOL?*

... MOST *PUP*-ULAR!

$$\frac{\text{BROTH} + \text{DAYTIME TV}}{\text{SOUP OPERA}}$$

WHICH **DAY** OF THE WEEK IS **BAZOOKA JOE'S** FAVORITE?

 ... **CHEWS**-DAY!

WHAT DID THE **PROFESSOR** SAY TO THE **OTHER PROFESSOR** AT HIS **RETIREMENT PARTY?**

... "KEEP IN **TEACH!**"

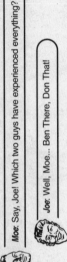

WHY IS IT **EXPENSIVE** TO CALL **ITALY** ON YOUR **CELL PHONE?**

... BECAUSE OF THE **ROMAN CHARGES!**

WHAT WOULD **YOU** CALL **SCOOBY-DOO** IF HE WASN'T **HOUSE BROKEN?**

... SCOOBY-**DOODIE!**

WHICH **RESTAURANT** SERVES **PIES** THAT YOU **WEAR** ON YOUR **HEAD?**

... PIZZA **HAT!**

HERE DOES A **SQUIRREL** LIKE TO **SHOP?**

... AT **WAL-NUT-MART!**

NINE PLAYERS + A STEER

―――――――――――

BASE-BULL

WHAT DID THE *BANANA* SAY TO THE *PEA?*

... "LET'S *SPLIT!*"

HAT KIND OF *COMPUTER* DOES A *POLE VAULTER* USE?

... A *LEAP* TOP!

 @ MAD ADD JOKE!

A PIMPLE
+ A VIDEO GAME
———————————
POCKMAN

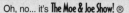
Oh, no... it's **The Moe & Joe Show!** ®

Moe: Say, Joe! How do you dress up your eyes?

Joe: Well, Moe... you clothes them!

WHAT'S THE BEST PIECE OF **GYM EQUIPMENT** FOR **WEIGHT LOSS?**

... A TRAMPO-**LEAN!**

WHERE DID THE **HAND** LIKE TO **EAT?**

... AT A **FIST**-FOOD RESTAURANT!

HAT DOES A **MONSTER** LIKE TO **DRINK** OUT OF?

... A **FRANKEN**-STEIN!

WHAT DID THE **WITCH** DO WHEN ELECTED TO **OFFICE?**

 ... SHE MADE **SWEEPING CHANGES!**

HICH **RELATIVES** ALWAYS LIVE **UPSTAIRS?**

... **STEP**-PARENTS!

WHAT KIND OF *VEHICLE* DOES A *LUMBERJACK* DRIVE?

... A *FIR* BY *FIR*!

WHAT KIND OF *VEHICLE* DOES *DRACULA* DRIVE?

 ... A *FEAR* BY *FEAR*!

HAT KIND OF *VEHICLE* DOES *TIGER WOODS* DRIVE?

... A *FORE* BY *FORE*!

A PIG
+ A RIDDLE
——————
A DIRTY JOKE

Oh, no... it's **The Moe & Joe Show!** ® *Moe:* Say, Joe! What did the cartoonist's bumper sticker say?

Joe: Well, Moe... "How Am I Drawing?"

WHAT DID *HONG KONG* SAY TO *TAIWAN?*

... "I CAUGHT YOU *PEKING!*"

WHY DO *WITCHES* LIKE TO RIDE *BROOMS?*

... VACUUM CLEANERS ARE TOO *HEAVY!*

OW DOES A *CAR* RUN WITHOUT AN *ENGINE?*

... YOU JUST PUT A *HILL UNDER IT!*

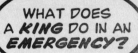
WHAT DOES A **KING** DO IN AN **EMERGENCY?**

... STOP, DROP AND **RULE!**

WHAT DOES A **BASEBALL PLAYER** KEEP ON HIS **DOORSTEP?**

... A WELCOME **MITT!**

WHAT WOULD **SANTA** SAY IF HE WERE A **PIRATE?**

... **"YO**-HO-HO-HO!"

Oh, no... it's **The Moe & Joe Show!** ® *Moe*: Say, Joe! Why did the silly man work in the candy factory?

 Joe: Well, Moe... he was a nut-job!

WHAT IS A **DOG'S PHILOSOPHY?**

... "THE **WORST THINGS** IN LIFE ARE **FLEAS!**"

$$\frac{\text{A FRUIT} + \text{A GYMNAST}}{\text{BANANA SPLIT}}$$

WHAT DO **YOU** CALL A **POSITIVE THINKING KANGAROO?**

... A **HOP**-TIMIST!

Oh, no... it's **The Moe & Joe Show!** ®

Moe: Say, Joe! Where does a weight lifter like to eat?

 Joe: Well, Moe... at the buff-et!

WHAT'S A *TELETUBBY'S* FAVORITE *CANDY?*

... A *LAA-LAA-POP!*

WHAT **SMELLS** THE **MOST** IN A **GARBAGE DUMP?**

... THE **NOSE!**

WHICH **GAME** HAS **ELEVEN PLAYERS** ON A TEAM KICKING A **LOLLIPOP?**

... **SUCK**-ER!

Oh, no... it's **The Moe & Joe Show!** ® **Moe**: Say, Joe! What do twins travel on?

Joe: Well, Moe... a twain!

WHAT DOES A *BASEBALL PITCHER* THROW AFTER NOT *EATING?*

... *A FAST BALL!*

HOW DO YOU SAY *BATHROOM* IN FRENCH?

... "*BATHROOM* IN FRENCH!"

WHAT DOES A *SNAKE* WEAR WITH A *TUXEDO?*

... A *BOA*-TIE!

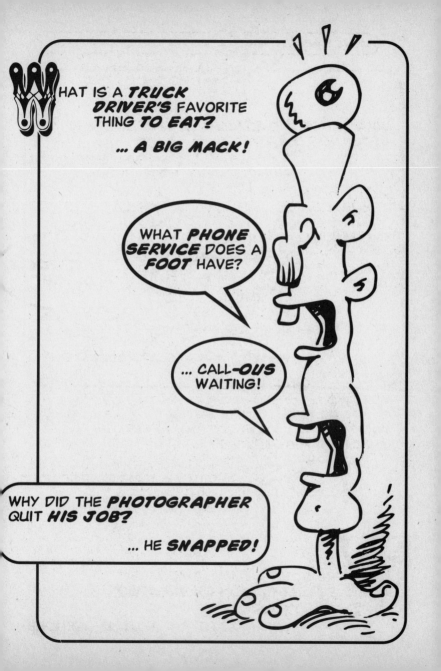

WHY DID THE **MATCH** QUIT PLAYING **BASEBALL?**

YOE!

... HE WAS ALWAYS **STRIKING** OUT!

WHAT DID THE **TARGET** SAY AFTER THE **ARCHER** MISSED HIM?

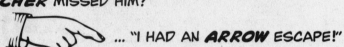

... "I HAD AN **ARROW** ESCAPE!"

WHERE DOES A **GIRL GHOST** GO TO GET READY FOR A **DATE?**

... TO THE **SCARE**-DRESSER!

WHAT CAN *YOU* JOIN TO EARN LOTS OF *BREAD?*

... THE *TOAST* GUARD!

WHAT DID *SPIDERMAN* DO WHEN HE BORROWED THE *BATMOBILE?*

... HE TOOK IT FOR A *SPIN!*

WHAT *TOPPING* DOES A *RAZOR* LIKE ON *STRAWBERRY SHORTCAKE?*

... *SHAVING CREAM!*

Oh, no... it's **The Moe & Joe Show!** ® *Moe*: Say, Joe! What do you call a comedian at the beach?

 Joe: Well, Moe... a laugh-guard!

WHY DID THE **APPLE** GO TO THE **DOCTOR?**

... BECAUSE HE FELT **ROTTEN TO THE CORE!**

WHAT DO **YOU** CALL AN **OSTRICH** THAT HAS **LOST** HIS **MONEY?**

... AN OST-**POOR!**

HAT DOES A **GHOST** DO WHEN SHE **GETS INTO** A **CAR?**

... FASTENS HER **SHEET** BELT!

Oh, no... it's **The Moe & Joe Show!** ® *Moe*: Say, Joe! What's the most artistic type of bridge?

 Joe: Well, Moe... a drawbridge!

WHERE DO *MONSTERS* GO TO *SCHOOL?*

... *GOON*-IVERSITIES!

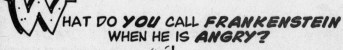

WHAT DO *YOU* CALL *FRANKENSTEIN* WHEN HE IS *ANGRY?*

... FRANK-*INCENSED!*

 @ **MAD JOKE!**

$$\frac{WINTER + DRACULA}{FROSTBITE}$$

Star-Spangled BANTER

DEPARTMENT

WHAT IS A **SHEEP'S** FAVORITE STATE?

EWE-TAH!

HAT IS A **LION'S** FAVORITE STATE?

MAIN!

WHAT **STATE** IS THE **LOUDEST?**

YELL-OWARE!

WHAT IS A **FRIENDLIEST** STATE?

O-HI-O!

WHAT IS A **ROW-BOAT'S** FAVORITE STATE?

OAR-EGON!

WHAT **STATE** GOES TO THE **DOCTOR** ALOT?

ILL-INOIS!

WHICH **STATE** IS THE BEST **DANCER?**

KAN-KAN SAS!

WHAT IS **BARBIE'S** FAVORITE STATE?

KEN-TUCKY!

HAT **STATE** IS THE **TINIEST?**

MINI-SOTA!

WHAT IS A PIECE OF **PAPER'S** FAVORITE STATE?

PENCIL-VANIA!

WHAT IS A **PAIR** OF **EYEGLASSES** FAVORITE STATE?

EYE-DAHO!

WHAT STATE CAN YOU **WALK ON?**

FLOOR-IDA!

WHAT IS A **CRAYON'S** FAVORITE STATE?

COLOR-ADO!

WHAT STATE TAKES THE MOST **SHOWERS?**

WASK-INGTON!

WHAT IS A **GEEKS** FAVORITE STATE?

NEW-DORK!

WHERE DID THE **COW** TAKE HIS **DATE** ON **SATURDAY NIGHT?**

... TO THE **MOO**-VIES!

WHAT DOES A **SALESMAN** MAKE HIS **PHONE CALLS** ON?

... A **SELL** PHONE!

WHAT DID THE **MOMMY CREDIT CARD** SAY TO THE **KID CREDIT CARD?**

 ... "**SWIPE** YOUR NOSE!"

WHAT DID THE **SPORTS ANNOUNCER** SAY AS THE **HOT DOG** WON THE **RACE?**

... "WE HAVE A **WIENER!**"

HY WAS THE **MAMA DEER** ANNOYED WITH THE **PAPA DEER?**

... HE WAS A **BUCK-SEAT DRIVER!**

$$\frac{\text{A MALL} + \text{A PATRIOTIC ZEBRA}}{\text{STORES AND STRIPES}}$$

WHAT DO *YOU* CALL A *COWBOY* WITH *COTTON* IN HIS *EARS?*

... A *HEAR*-LESS HORSEMAN!

WHAT IS THE MOST *INQUISITIVE* STATE?

... *WHY*-OMING!

@ MAD ADD JOKE!

RAZOR BLADES + BUREAU

A SHARP DRESSER

Oh, no... it's **The Moe & Joe Show!** ® **Moe**: Say, Joe! What kind of snake tells on his brother?

 Joe: Well, Moe... a tattle-snake!

Joe: Well, Moe... "Yo-Yo-Yo!"

WHAT KIND OF *FURNITURE* DO *INSECTS* LIKE?

... *ANT*-TIQUES!

ON WHAT KIND OF *BED* DO YOU HIT YOUR *HEAD?*

... A *BONK*-BED!

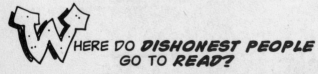

HERE DO *DISHONEST PEOPLE* GO TO *READ?*

... THE *LIE*-BRARY!

WHAT DO *YOU* GET WHEN YOU *CROSS* AN *ELEPHANT* WITH A *GOLDFISH?*

... A *FISHBOWL* THAT NEEDS TO BE CLEANED *DAILY!*

HAT'S A *COW'S* FAVORITE *SONG?*

... "JINGLE *BULLS!*"

FAIRY TALES
+ ARITHMETIC
―――――――――――
MYTH-EMATICS

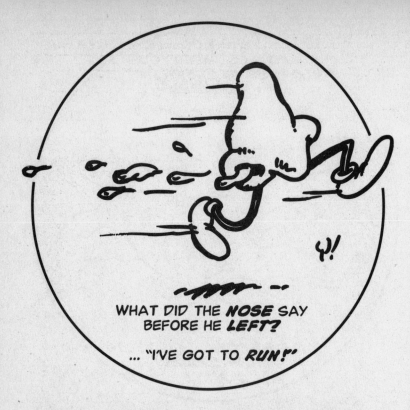

WHAT DID THE *NOSE* SAY
BEFORE HE *LEFT?*

... "I'VE GOT TO *RUN!*"

WHAT DO *YOU* CALL A *LITTLE TOE* DOING A
SOMERSAULT?

 ... A *TOOTSIE* ROLL!

 MICKEY MOUSE
+ A LONG BATH
————————————
SQUEAKY-CLEAN

Oh, no... it's **The Moe & Joe Show!** ® *Moe*: Say, Joe! Who did the Big Bad Wolf marry?

 Joe: Well, Moe... Little Wed Riding Hood!

WHY DOESN'T *TARZAN'S MONKEY* LIKE TO PLAY *GAMES?*

... BECAUSE *CHEETAHS* NEVER WIN!

WHAT DID THE *BOAT* DO WHEN IT WAS FEELING *SICK?*

... IT WENT TO THE *DOCK*-TOR!

HY DID THE *ZOO KEEPER* FEEL HE NEEDED TO WEAR *GLASSES* WHILE FEEDING THE *LEOPARDS?*

... BECAUSE HE HAD *SPOTS* IN FRONT OF HIS *EYES!*

WHAT'S THE **DIFFERENCE** BETWEEN **AUSTRALIA** AND A **MUSHROOM?**

... **LOTS OF THINGS!**

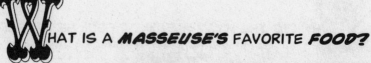WHAT IS A **MASSEUSE'S** FAVORITE **FOOD?**

 ... BABY-BACK **RUBS!**

WHY DO **SPIDERS** MAKE GOOD **OUTFIELDERS?**

... BECAUSE THEY CAN **CATCH FLIES!**

WHAT DID THE **ADMIRER** OF **IMPRESSIONIST PAINTINGS** SAY TO THE **MUSEUM GUIDE?**

... "SHOW ME THE **MONET!**"

@ **MAD JOKE!**

A LADDER
+ NOSTRIL JEWELRY
――――――――――
A NOSE RUNG

HOW DOES A **BEAR**
FEEL AFTER A **LONG WINTER'S NAP?**

... **DEN**-ERGETIC!

WHAT DOES **WINNIE THE POOH** SAY WHEN HE
RETURNS TO HIS **TREE?**

... "HONEY, I'M HOME!"

@ **MAD**
ADD
JOKE!

PUBLIC TRANSPORTATION
+ A BUMBLE BEE
———————————
A GREYHOUND BUZZ

Oh, no... it's **The Moe & Joe Show!** ® *Moe*: Say, Joe! What's big, brown, and coated?

 Joe: Well, Moe... a chocolate bear!

WHAT DID ONE **MOUNTAIN** SAY TO THE
OTHER **MOUNTAIN?**

... "DO THESE JEANS
MAKE MY **BUTTE** LOOK FAT?"

HAT DO **YOU** DO AFTER **NODDING OFF TO
SLEEP** ON AN **AIRPLANE?**

... YOU **RETURN YOUR HEAD TO ITS
UPRIGHT POSITION!**

WHAT DID THE **DOLPHIN** SAY AFTER THE **SHARK** SPLASHED HIM?

... "YOU DID THAT ON **PORPOISE!**"

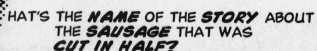

WHAT'S THE **NAME** OF THE **STORY** ABOUT THE **SAUSAGE** THAT WAS **CUT IN HALF?**

... "HOW THE **WURST** WAS ONE!"

IS THAT *GREEN JELLO* ON YOUR *LIP?*

... NO, IT'S-*NOT!*

WHAT DID *BUGS BUNNY* BUY FOR HIS *GIRLFRIEND?*

... A 20 *CARROT* DIAMOND RING!

@MAD ADD JOKE!

$$\frac{\text{ORANGE BEAR} + \text{FLUFFY DOG}}{\text{WINNIE THE POOH-DLE}}$$

HOW DO *YOU* GET YOUR *DOG* TO *EAT UNDERWATER?*

... FEED HIM *GUPPY* CHOW!

WHAT WAS THE *POOR LOCKSMITH* ALWAYS *LOOKING FOR?*

... *THE KEY TO SUCCESS!*

A MONSTER
+ SOCCER PLAYER
―――――――――
A GHOUL-IE

Oh, no... it's **The Moe & Joe Show!** ® *Moe*: Say, Joe! Which drink is always losing its temper?

Joe: Well, Moe... Snap-ple!

WHAT DOES A **TYRANNOSAURUS REX** LIKE TO EAT FOR **BREAKFAST?**

... AN **EGG-O-SAURUS!**

WHAT KIND OF A **DOG** USES A **CELL PHONE?**

... A **WIRE-LESS TERRIER!**

WHAT HAPPENS TO A **MCDONALD'S RESTAURANT** DURING AN **EARTHQUAKE?**

... **FALLEN ARCHES!**

WHAT KIND OF *BOOK* DOES A *BUG* LIKE TO *READ?*

... ROM-*ANTS* NOVELS!

WHAT DOES A *JIGSAW PUZZLE* DO AFTER A *BAD EXPERIENCE?*

 ... TRIES TO *PICK UP THE PIECES!*

WHERE IS THE **BEST PLACE** TO GIVE YOUR FRIEND A **HIGH FIVE?**

... **PALM** BEACH!

WHY DID THE **TOILET** GO TO THE **DOCTOR?**

... IT WAS FEELING **FLUSHED!**

ONE-WHEELED BIKE
+ YELLOW VEGGIE
_____
UNI-CORN

WHAT DOES A *FENCE* LIKE TO *READ*?

... *PEEP*-HOLE MAGAZINE!

WHAT DO *YOU* CALL IT WHEN A *RUGRAT* THROWS UP?

... UP-*CHUCKIE!*

@ MAD ADD JOKE!

SATURDAY NIGHT FEVER + A BEE'S HOME
———————————————
STAYIN' A HIVE

WHAT'S A **PRACTICAL JOKER'S** FAVORITE **FOOD?**

... PRANK-FURTERS!

WHAT DID THE **JOURNALISM TEACHER** TELL THE **STUDENT** WHO WAS DOING HIS **HOMEWORK** IN **SCHOOL?**

... "STOP PICKING YOUR **NEWS** IN CLASS!"

TOP OF THE WORLD
+ OLYMPIC ATHLETE
─────────────────
NORTH POLE VAULTER

Oh, no... it's **The Moe & Joe Show!** ®   *Moe*: Say, Joe! What's a cow's favorite day?

Joe: Well, Moe... Moos-day!

WHY WAS THE *POODLE* SO *HAPPY?*

... HE GOT A *NEW LEASH ON LIFE!*

WHERE DID THE *COMPUTER* LIKE TO *GO* ON *FRIDAY NIGHTS?*

... TO THE *DISK*-O!

WHAT DID *ONE TREE* SAY TO THE OTHER *TREE* AT THE *END* OF THE *DAY?*

... *"I'VE GOTTA LEAVE!"*

WHAT MAKES AN *INSECT* SMELL *GOOD?*

*... **FLEA**-ODERANT!*

WHAT DO *YOU* GET WHEN YOU CROSS *DRACULA* WITH A *GOOSE?*

*... A **COUNT DOWN!***

@ MAD ADD JOKE!

$$\frac{\text{2 INSECTS} + \text{ROYALTY}}{\text{BEE-BEE KING}}$$

WHAT'S A **MONSTER'S** FAVORITE *ICE CREAM FLAVOR?*

YOE!

... ***SHOCK***-OLATE!

WHAT IS **PEBBLES'** FAVORITE *ICE CREAM FLAVOR?*

... ***ROCKY*** ROAD!

TOILET
+ A SPACE HERO
_____
FLUSH GORDON

WHERE DOES A **CARPENTER** FILE HIS **WOOD?**

... UNDER THE LETTER **"W"**!

Oh, no... it's *The Moe & Joe Show!* ®

Moe: Say, Joe! What did the bathroom scale tell the feather?

Joe: Well, Moe... "No weigh!"

HAT IS A *TEACHER'S* FAVORITE *ICE CREAM FLAVOR?*

... ***CHALK*-O-**LATE!

HOW DID THE **SWISS CHEESE** TREAT THE **CHEDDAR?**

... WITH A **HOLIER**-THAN-THOU ATTITUDE!

HY DID THE **COMEDIAN** LOVE **HALLOWEEN?**

... BECAUSE OF ALL THE **JOKE**-O'-LANTERNS!

WHAT DO **YOU** CALL A **DECK OF CARDS** WITH **4,529** CARDS?

... A **BIG DEAL!**

WHAT KIND OF **TREE** LIKES TO VISIT THE **OCEAN?**

... A **BEECH** TREE!

WHAT'S THE BEST WAY **TO PASS A TEST** IN **MUSIC CLASS?**

... STUDY YOUR **NOTES!**

PRECIPITATION
+ BABY CHICKEN
_____
A RAIN CHICK

WHAT DO *YOU* CALL A *DOG* THAT *FARTS* A LOT?

YOE!

... A *FARTY* ANIMAL!

WHAT'S THE *MOST ROMANTIC THING* ABOUT THE *OCEAN?*

... WHEN THE BOATS *HUG* THE SHORE!

@ **MAD ADD** JOKE!®

TINY FRUIT
+ MOVIE STAR
―――――――――
CHERRY PITT

WHO BRINGS *TOYS* TO *KIDS* AND LIVES AT THE *BEACH?*

... SAND-A CLAUS!

WHY WASN'T THE *COMPUTER* ALLOWED TO *DRIVE?*

... BECAUSE IT KEPT *CRASHING!*

HAT HAPPENED AFTER THE *LEOPARD* GOT *HIT* ON THE *HEAD?*

... HE SAW *SPOTS!*

IN WHAT **CITY** DO PEOPLE **EAT** THE **MOST EGGS?**

 ... NEW **YOLK!**

$$\frac{INSECTS + KING KONG}{GI\text{-}ANTS}$$

WHAT DID THE **TELEVISION** SAY
TO THE **REMOTE CONTROL?**

... "DON'T GO **CHANGIN'!**"

MATH OR SCIENCE
+ BOZO
―――――――――――――
CLASS CLOWN

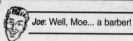
WHY COULDN'T THE *HUMMINGBIRD* HUM?

... BECAUSE HE WAS *HUM-SICK!*

WHAT DO *YOU* CALL A *LITTLE SNEEZE?*

... "MUCH *ACHOO* ABOUT NOTHING!"

WHEN IS THE *INVISIBLE MAN* VISIBLE?

... WHEN HE HAS A *KID,* HE'S *A-PARENT!*

BODY OF WATER
+ CUTTING TOOL
_____
SEA SAW

WHAT IS THE *LAZIEST SHOE?*

... A *LOAFER!*

WHY DID THE *DOUGHNUT MAKER* GO *BANKRUPT?*

... HE COULDN'T GET OUT OF THE *HOLE!*

HAT DO *YOU* GET WHEN YOU PUT AN *ELEPHANT* AND A *PEANUT* BETWEEN *TWO SLICES OF BREAD?*

... A *PEANUT ELEPHANT SANDWICH!*

WHAT DOES A *HEAD OF HAIR* EAT FOR *BREAKFAST?*

 ... *DANDRUFF* FLAKES!

HOW CAN **YOU** START THE **DAY**
WITH A **SMILE?**

... EAT **GRIN**-OLA!

HAT DID THE **LADDER** DO ON
DECEMBER 31ˢᵀ?

... HE **RUNG** IN **THE
NEW YEAR!**

 A VEGETABLE
+ A TELEFLORIST
———————————
A CALL-A-FLOWER

WHAT DO *YOU* DO IF YOU HAVE A *RING* IN YOUR *NOSE?*

... YOU'D BETTER *ANSWER IT!*

WHAT DO *YOU* GET WHEN YOU CROSS A *CARTOON DOG* WITH THE *MORNING MIST?*

 ... *SCOOBY-DEW!*

WHAT DID ONE *HAMBURGER PATTY* SAY TO THE OTHER *HAMBURGER PATTY?*

... "WE'RE ON A *ROLL!*"

WHAT DO *YOU* CALL A *MAN* WHO WORKS IN THE *ALPHBET SOUP FACTORY?*

... A MAN OF *LETTERS!*

HAT IS A *BATHTUB'S* FAVORITE *DESSERT?*

... A *CAKE* OF *SOAP!*

 A FATHER + A FLOWER

—————————

A POPPY

WHAT DOES A *GHOST* LIKE TO *PLAY WITH* WHILE IN *AUSTRALIA?*

... A ***BOO*-MERANG!**

WHAT DID THE *CAT* GIVE THE *DOG* FOR HIS *BIRTHDAY?*

... ***COLLIE*-FLOWERS!**

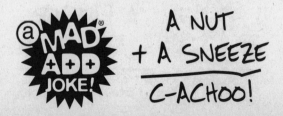

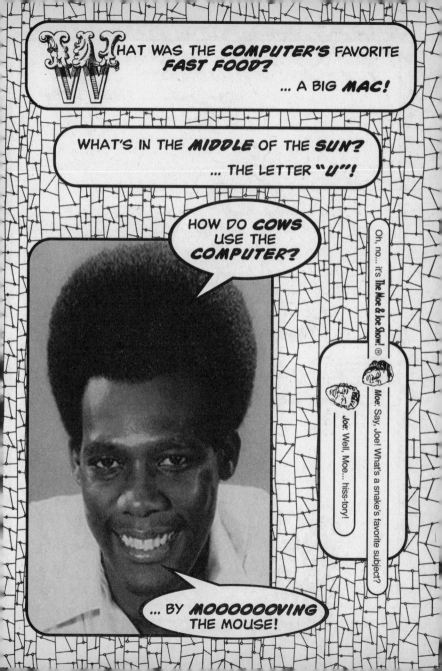

WHAT DO **YOU** GET IF YOU CROSS
THE FLASH WITH A **TOILET?**

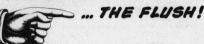 ... **THE FLUSH!**

WHY DID THE **MAN** GET A **BARGAIN**
ON HIS **BOAT?**

... IT WAS A **SALE** BOAT!

 $$\frac{\text{24 EXPOSURES} + \text{DAFFY}}{\text{KO-DUCK}}$$

Oh, no... it's **The Moe & Joe Show!** ® **Moe:** Say, Joe! What does a wolf do?

Joe: Well, Moe... steal wool!

 OW DO **YOU** GET A **MONSTER** OUT OF YOUR **LUNCH BOX?**

... THE SAME WAY YOU GOT HIM **IN!**

WHAT'S **ORANGE** AND GOES **"SLAM-SLAM-SLAM-SLAM"?**

... A **FOUR-DOOR CARROT!**

Moe: Say, Joe! What do you always find at the end of a trail?

Joe: Well, Moe... the letter "L"!

WHAT PART OF A *CAR* LOOKS MOST LIKE AN *ELEPHANT?*

... THE *TRUNK!*

WHAT DOES A *CENSUS TAKER* DO IF HE CATCHES *FIRE?*

... STOP, DROP AND *POLL!*

HAT DO *YOU* CALL IT WHEN YOUR *DOG* SWALLOWS YOUR *CLOCK?*

... *ALARMING!*

WHAT HAS *THREE HORNS* AND *DRIBBLES* A *BALL?*

... A *THREE HORNED BALL DRIBBLER!*

$$\frac{\text{A LIAR} + \text{A CANDY BAR}}{\text{TRUTH DECAY}}$$

WHAT DOES A *YO-YO* DO ON *VACATION?*

... IT *UNWINDS!*

AN UNSINKABLE BOAT + ROMAN CLOTHING

TI-TUNIC

WHAT DO **YOU** GET WHEN YOU CROSS A **SPRINTER** WITH **A COMEDIAN?**

... A **RUNNING JOKE!**

IN WHAT **ROOM** DO YOU MAKE **PORRIDGE?**
... IN A **MUSH**-ROOM!

DID **YOU** HEAR THAT **DRACULA** AND **WOLVERINE** HAD A **FIGHT?**

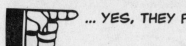 ... YES, THEY FOUGHT **TOOTH AND NAIL!**

WHAT'S **BLACK** AND **YELLOW** AND GOES *"BUZZ-BUZZ"*?

... NONE OF YOUR **BEES**-NESS!

HY IS **SPIDERMAN** OFTEN MISTAKEN FOR **DAFFY DUCK?**

... THEY BOTH HAVE **WEBBED FEET!**

Oh, no... it's **The Moe & Joe Show!** ® *Moe*: Say, Joe! What's Batman's favorite soup?

 Joe: Well, Moe... alpha-bat soup!

WHAT EATS *PEANUTS* AND SINGS *"THE STAR SPANGLED BANNER"*?

... A *PATRIOTIC ELEPHANT!*

HY DID THE *MILLIONAIRE* TAKE SUCH *GOOD CARE* OF HIS *PET?*

... BECAUSE IT WAS A *GOLD FISH!*

PLACE TO EAT
+ CHEERLEADER
─────────────────
RESTAU-RAH-RAH-NT

WHICH **FINGER** DO **YOU** USE TO TURN TO THE **END** OF A **BOOK?**

 ... THE **INDEX** FINGER!

WHAT DOES **SNOOPY** LIKE TO EAT AT **SNACKTIME?**

... **CHARLIE BROWN**-IES!

Oh, no... it's **The Moe & Joe Show!** ® *Moe*: Say, Joe! Why did the goof eat his flashlight?

 Joe: Well, Moe... he wanted a light dinner!

WHAT DID THE **LOG** SAY TO THE **ASHES?**

... "**YOU'RE FIRED!**"

YOE!

WHAT HAPPENS WHEN THE **GREEN GIANT** DIVES INTO THE **RED SEA?**

... HE GETS **WET!**

a **MAD ÷ JOKE!**

DRACULA
+ AN ARTIST
――――――――
DRAWING BLOOD!

WHAT DOES A *SHIP* SAY WHEN IT'S *COMING* INTO THE *HARBOR?*

... "WHAT'S UP *DOCK!*"

WHICH *LITTLE GIRL* ROBBED FROM THE *RICH* AND *GAVE* TO THE *POOR* ON HER WAY TO HER *GRANDMOTHER'S HOUSE?*

... LITTLE RED *ROBBIN'* HOOD!

HAT DO *YOU* TELL AN *UPTIGHT SNOWMAN?*

... "*CHILL OUT!*"

WHAT DOES A **CAT** HAVE THAT **NOTHING ELSE** HAS?

... **KITTENS!**

WHY DID THE **SUN** GET SUCH **GOOD GRADES** IN **SCHOOL?**

... BECAUSE IT'S VERY **BRIGHT!**

 Oh, no... it's **The Moe & Joe Show!** ® **Moe**: Say, Joe! Where did Beethoven write his sonatas?

 Joe: Well, Moe... in a note-book!

WHAT IS A **CAN'S FAVORITE SPORT?**

... **TIN**-NIS!

 HAT KIND OF **COMEDY ROUTINE** DOES A **WITCH** PERFORM?

... BROOM **SCHTICK!**

WHY WAS THE *ROSE* SO *SMART?*

... HE WAS A *BUDDING* GENIUS!

A+

HY DO *FLEAS* ALWAYS GET SO *HUNGRY* BETWEEN *BREAKFAST* AND *DINNER?*

... 'CAUSE THERE'S NO SUCH THING AS A *FLEA* LUNCH!

@ MAD ADD JOKE!

A VULCAN
+ PASTA
――――――
SPOCK-GHETTI

HOW DO **CLOWNS** SEND
COMPUTER MESSAGES?

... **GLEE**-MAIL!

WHERE CAN **YOU** READ THE **ADVENTURES**
OF **CASPER?**

 ... IN A COMIC **BOO**-K!

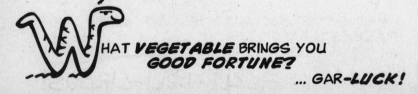

HAT **VEGETABLE** BRINGS YOU
GOOD FORTUNE?

... GAR-**LUCK!**

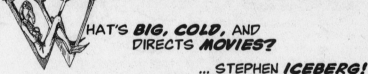

WHAT'S **BIG, COLD,** AND DIRECTS **MOVIES?**

... STEPHEN **ICEBERG!**

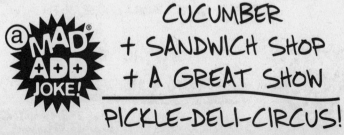

@ **MAD ADD** JOKE!®

CUCUMBER
+ SANDWICH SHOP
+ A GREAT SHOW
─────────────────
PICKLE-DELI-CIRCUS!

WHY COULDN'T THE *HUMAN TORCH*
GET *MARRIED?*

... HE COULDN'T FIND HIS *MATCH!*

WHY DID THE *WITCH* FLY ALONG
THE *SEASHORE?*

... SHE WANTED A *BROOM* WITH A VIEW!

@ MAD
+ + +
JOKE!

SONIC BLAST
+ LAWN GROOMING TOOL

SONIC THE HEDGECLIPPER

WHAT KIND OF **MUSIC** DOES A **GHOST** LIKE?

... **HAUNTING** MELODIES!

WHAT DO **YOU** CALL A **BLIND BUCK**?

I HAVE **NO-EYE-DEER!**

Oh, no... it's **The Moe & Joe Show!** ®

Moe: Say, Joe! What do you call it when your plane stops in Hawaii?

Joe: Well, Moe... a Lei-over!

WHAT DO **YOU** CALL A **POSITIVE THINKING ANIMAL** FROM **AUSTRALIA?**

... A **CAN-DO-GAROO!**

HERE DO *HUMMINGBIRDS* LIKE TO *SHOP?*

... THE *HUM* DEPOT!

WHAT DO *YOU* CALL A *STUPID GARBAGE CONTAINER?*

... A *DUMB*-STER!

WHAT KIND OF *FISH* DRINKS *QUICKLY?*

... A *GULP-y!*

@ MAD ADD JOKE!

STORMY WEATHER
+ A FRENCH BOYFRIEND
———————————
A RAIN-BEAU

WHAT DID THE *DIRECTOR* SAY AFTER MAKING THE *MUMMY* MOVIE?

... "IT'S A *WRAP!*"

WHY DID THE *DRIVER* ROLL DOWN HIS *WINDOW?*

... BECAUSE HE *PASSED* THE *GAS STATION!*

Oh, no... it's **The Moe & Joe Show!** ® *Moe:* Say, Joe! What was the shoe's favorite sport?

 Joe: Well, Moe... sock-er!

HOW DO *DOGS* BUY *NEW CARS?*

... THEY *LEASH* THEM!

 HICH *SUPERHERO GROUP* PROTECTS THE *NATIONAL FORESTS?*

... THE JUSTICE *LOG* OF AMERICA!

WHY WAS THE *FISH* SO *UNIQUE?*

... HE MARCHED TO THE *TUN-A* HIS OWN DRUMMER!

WHAT DOES A *HOUSE*
LIKE TO *DRINK?*

... *ROOF* BEER!

@ **MAD ADD JOKE!**

$$\frac{\text{RUNNING SHOES} + \text{A LIBRARY}}{\text{REE-BOOKS}}$$

HOW DID THE LETTER *"E"* DROWN?

... IT FOUND ITSELF IN THE
MIDDLE OF THE *OCEAN!*

DID **YOU** HEAR THAT THE **HUMAN TORCH** IS **LOSING WEIGHT?**

... YEAH, HE'S **BURNING CALORIES!**

 Oh, no... it's **The Moe & Joe Show!** ® **Moe**: Say, Joe! What did the cow say on January 1st?

 Joe: Well, Moe... "Happy Moo Year!"

WHY DOES **DRACULA** KEEP HIS **MOUTH SHUT?**

 ... BECAUSE SILENCE IS **GHOUL-DEN!**

WHY DID THE **WORM** BURROW
INTO HIS **COMPUTER?**

... IT WAS AN **APPLE!**

WHAT'S A
ROBOT'S
FAVORITE
SNACK?

... **NUTS
AND
BOLTS!**

WHAT IS **PINK, COLD,** AND
VERY DANGEROUS?

... **SHARK-INFESTED**
RASPBERRY ICE CREAM!

A DIRTY JOKE
+ A BAD BOWLER
—————————————
A MIND THAT'S IN THE GUTTER

WHAT DO *YOU* CALL A *TIRED COW* GRAZING IN YOUR *BACKYARD?*

... *A YAWN MOOER!*

HERE DOES A *FISH* LIKE TO *SLEEP?*

... IN A *RIVER* BED!

 FELIX THE CAT
+ A DOLPHIN
———————————
PURR-PUSS

WHAT DOES **NEW YORK CITY** HAVE THAT **NO OTHER CITY** HAS?

 ... **NEW YORKERS!**

WHAT **ANIMAL** SHOULDN'T **YOU** INVITE TO A **PARADE?**

... A **RAIN**-DEER!

WHERE DO *COMEDIANS* GO WHEN THEY'RE *SICK?*

... TO THE *HE-HE*-MERGENCY ROOM!

WHAT IS A *GOLFER'S* FAVORITE *DRINK?*

... ICED *TEE!*

@ MAD ADD JOKE!

DRACULA
+ A GIRAFFE
―――――――――
TRUE LOVE

WHY DID THE **TEACHER** QUIT HER **JOB?**

... SHE WAS **SCHOOL BORED!**

WHY WAS THE **REFRIGERATOR** TIRED?

... BECAUSE IT HAD BEEN **RUNNING ALL DAY!**

A GHOST

+ FRUIT

——————

BOO-BERRIES

Oh, no... it's **The Moe & Joe Show!** ® *Moe*: Say, Joe! Was Bruce Wayne married?

 Joe: Well, Moe... no, he was a bat-chelor!

WHAT DO *YOU* CALL IT WHEN *DRACULA* STAYS *AWAKE* FOR *24 HOURS?*

... AN *ALL DAY SUCKER!*

WHAT IS A *PODIATRIST'S* FAVORITE *CHANNEL?*

... THE *FOOT* NETWORK!

WHO WAS THE *SHEEP'S* FAVORITE *SUPERHERO?*

... *BAAA-TMAN!*

HAT'S THE *BEST THING* TO PUT ON YOUR *BED* ON A *REALLY HOT DAY?*

... A *SHEET* OF *ICE!*

WHY DO *UNDERPANTS* LAST SO *LONG?*

... BECAUSE THEY ARE NEVER *WORN OUT!*

Oh, no... it's **The Moe & Joe Show!** ® *Moe*: Say, Joe! Why did the crossword seem confused?

 Joe: Well, Moe... because it was puzzled!

WHY SHOULDN'T **YOU** TRUST **BIG FEROCIOUS CATS** WITH **MANES?**

... BECAUSE THEY'RE ALWAYS **LION!**

HAT DID THE **SNOWSTORM** SAY TO THE **MOUNTAIN?**

... "DO YOU GET MY **DRIFT?**"

FRANKENSTEIN + COLONEL SANDERS

TERRI-FRIED

DOES A *ROTTING MUMMY* SMELL?

... IT *SPHINX*

WHY DID THE *EGG* BECOME A *COMEDIAN?*

... BECAUSE HE KNEW A LOT OF *YOLKS!*

HAT KIND OF *COMPUTER* DOES A *CYCLOPS* LIKE TO *USE?*

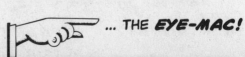 ... THE *EYE-MAC!*

WHAT'S in a NAME? DEPARTMENT

WHAT *BOY* LOVES *PICKLES?*

DILL-ON!

WHAT *GIRL* LOVES *KITTENS?*

CAT-HARINE!

WHAT *GIRL* HAS A REAL *SWEET TOOTH?*

CANDY!

WHAT *BOY* IS GOOD AT FIXING *FLAT TIRES?*

JACK!

WHAT **GIRL** COLLECTS MONEY FOR THE **NEEDY?**

CHARITY!

HAT **BOY** LIKES TO **LAY** IN FRONT OF THE **DOOR?**

MATT!

WHAT **BOY** HAS LOTS OF **PET FISH?**

GILL-BERT!

HAT **BOY** DRESSES IN LOTS OF **BRIGHT COLORS?**

HUE-Y!

HAT **GIRL** LIKES TO EAT **OYSTERS?**

PEARL!

HAT **BOY** LIKES TO **WORK OUT?**

GYM-Y!

WHY DID THE **BASKETBALL PLAYER** SNACK ON **COOKIES** AND **MILK?**

... BECAUSE HE LIKED TO **DUNK!**

$$\frac{\text{A STORM} + \text{A SNAKE}}{\text{A RAIN-BOA}}$$

WHAT KIND OF *MUSIC* DO *CONVICTS* LIKE?

... ROCK-N-*PAROLE!*

WHAT DO *TENNIS PLAYERS* AND *BUTLERS* HAVE IN *COMMON?*

... THEY *BOTH* LIKE TO *SERVE!*

Oh, no... it's *The Moe & Joe Show!* ®

Moe: Say, Joe! How did the oak tree feel after watching Woody Woodpecker?

Joe: Well, Moe... bored!

HAT DOES A *COBRA* WEAR ON HIS *FEET?*

 ... *SNAKE*-ERS!

WHAT DID **KING KONG** GET FOR
HIS **SPORTS CAR**?

... AN **APE**-CASSETTE PLAYER!

A COCONUT TREE
+ AIRPLANE
———————————
PALM PILOT

WHAT DID THE *TREE* SAY TO THE *BIRD?*

... *"LEAF* ME ALONE!"

WHAT DO *YOU* CALL A *CAT* IN A *RED SUIT* WHO RIDES IN A *SLEIGH?*

... *SANTA PAWS!*

WHERE DO *FUNNY DOCTORS* WORK?

... AT THE *HA*-SPITAL!

WHY WAS THE *FOOTBALL PLAYER* LATE FOR THE *GAME?*

... HE HAD TO *HIKE!*

WHAT HAPPENED WHEN THE *POTATO* GOT *PULLED OVER* BY THE *POLICE?*

... HE GOT A *SPUD*-DING TICKET!

WHAT DO **YOU** CALL A **COW** THAT GIVES **CHOCOLATE MILK?**

 ... AN **UDDER** DELIGHT!

WHAT DID THE **COMPUTER** SAY TO THE **FIREPLACE?**

... "**LOG ON!**"

Oh, no... it's **The Moe & Joe Show!** ® *Moe*: Say, Joe! What's a computer's favorite musical instrument?

 Joe: Well, Moe... the keyboard!

WHY DID THE *COMEDIAN* GO TO THE *DOCTOR?*

... BECAUSE HE FELT *FUNNY!*

WHAT DO *YOU* SAY ABOUT A *RABBIT* THAT TURNS INTO A *MONSTER?*

... *"HARE* TODAY, *GOON* TOMORROW!"

WHEN DO *DUCKS* HAVE *FOUR FEET?*

... WHEN THERE ARE *TWO DUCKS!*

 Oh, no... it's **The Moe & Joe Show!** ® *Moe:* Say, Joe! Where does a cow buy tools?

 Joe: Well, Moe... the herd-ware store!

WHO HAS **MANY CHILDREN** AND LIVES
IN A **HAUNTED HOUSE?**

... THE OLD WOMAN WHO LIVES IN A **BOO!**

HAT'S **BARNEY RUBBLE'S** FAVORITE
ROCK GROUP?

... THE **ROLLING STONES!**

Oh, no... it's **The Moe & Joe Show!** ®

Moe: Say, Joe! What do you call a guy who's always wearing gold?

Joe: Well, Moe... a yellow fellow!

WHAT **CABLE CHANNEL** DO **RAPPERS** LIKE BEST?

... **HB-YO!**

OW DO **YOU** START A **LETTER** TO A **MUMMY?**

... "**TOMB IT MAY CONCERN!**'

WHY DID THE **RHINO** PAINT HIS **TOENAILS YELLOW, BLUE, RED, GREEN,** AND **BROWN?**

... SO HE COULD HIDE IN THE **M&M BAG!**

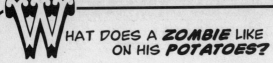

WHAT DOES A *ZOMBIE* LIKE ON HIS *POTATOES?*

... *GRAVE*-Y!

WHY DIDN'T *TARZAN* LEAVE THE *HUT?*

... BECAUSE IT'S A *JUNGLE* OUT THERE!

WHO'S THE *LEANEST* CARTOON ANIMAL?

... *SKINNY* THE POOH!

@ **MAD ADD** JOKE!

HOT DOGS + WEB SITE
————————————————
SAUSAGE LINKS

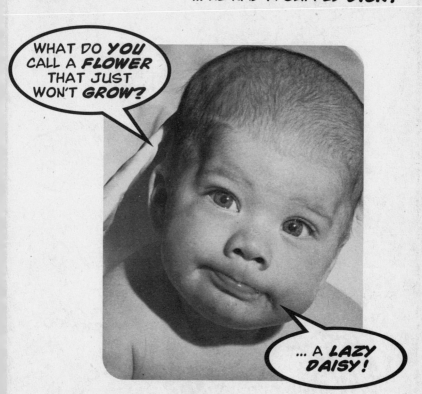

WHAT ALWAYS STAYS *HOT* IN THE *REFRIGERATOR?*

... *SALSA!*

WHAT *VEGETABLE* CAN *SEE?*

... GAR-*LOOK!*

WHAT DID THE *MONSTER* INSTALL ON HIS *COMPUTER?*

... A *SCREAM* SAVER!

a MAD ADD JOKE!

SMALL BUG + SMALL NAIL
——————————
TICK-TACK

WHY DO **YOU** HAVE TO BE **CAREFUL** WHEN YOU **CROSS** FROM ONE **STATE** INTO ANOTHER?

... BECAUSE OF THE **STATE LION!**

Oh, no... it's **The Moe & Joe Show!** ®

Moe: Say, Joe! How many peas are in one pail?

Joe: Well, Moe... one "P"!

WHAT **COLOR** IS THE **LOUDEST?**

... **YELL**-OW!

HY DIDN'T **PEOPLE** LAUGH AT THE **SCARECROW COMEDIAN?**

... BECAUSE HE TOLD **CORNY JOKES!**

WHY IS **PLASTIC MAN** SUCH A **LIAR?**

... HE **STRETCHES** THE TRUTH!

WHY DID **THOMAS EDISON** HAVE A **GOOD SENSE** OF **HUMOR?**

... HE MADE **LIGHT** OF EVERYTHING!

WHO TELLS **JOKES** AND LIVES IN **EMERALD CITY?**

... **THE WIZARD OF HA'S!**

A HERSHEY BAR + BULLWINKLE
―――――――――
CHOCOLATE MOOSE

WHAT'S THE BEST *MATERIAL* TO PUT ON A *CHAIR?*

... *SAT-IN!*

WHAT DOES *THE INVISIBLE MAN* USE TO CLEAN HIS *TOILET BOWL?*

... *VANISH!*

WHAT'S THE *BEST BREAD* TO USE WHEN YOU MAKE A *SWISS CHEESE SANDWICH?*

... *HOLE WHEAT!*

Oh, no... it's **The Moe & Joe Show!** ® *Moe*: Say, Joe! What type of instrument does a rabbit like to play?

 Joe: Well, Moe... hare-guitar!

Oh, no... it's **The Moe & Joe Show!** ® **Moe**: Say, Joe! What do monsters like in their chili?

Joe: Well, Moe... human beans!

WHY DID THE **BACHELOR** BUY A **CALENDAR?**

... HE WANTED LOTS OF **DATES!**

WHAT DO **YOU** SAY TO A **VAMPIRE** WHO WANTS TO **BITE** YOU?

 ... "THANKS, BUT NO **FANGS!**"

WHAT IS THE BEST WAY TO **CATCH** A **FISH** WITH A **COMPUTER?**

... USE THE INTER-**NET!**

WHAT IS ALWAYS *PRESENT* IN THE *MIDDLE* OF THE *NIGHT?*

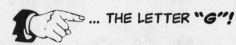 ... THE LETTER *"G"!*

WHY DID THE *MONKEY* QUIT HIS *JOB* AT THE *ZOO?*

... IT WAS *DRIVING* HIM *BANANAS!*

WHERE DOES THE **LITTLE MERMAID** LIKE TO **SLEEP?**

... IN A **WATERBED!**

HY DID THE **ARTIST** GO **FAR AWAY?**

... HE TOOK THE **EASEL** WAY OUT!

HOW DID THE **RUBBER BAND** GET TO THE **AIRPORT?**

... IN A **S T R E T C H** LIMO!

@ MAD ADD JOKE!

TYRANNOSAURUS REX
+ GYPSY
―――――――――――――
A DINO-SEER

WHICH **PART** OF YOUR **FACE** IS THE BIGGEST **GOSSIP?**

... **CHATTERING** TEETH!

AUTO MECHANIC + SALAD
WRENCH DRESSING

WHAT KIND OF *FOOD* ALWAYS HAS SOMETHING *NICE* TO SAY?

...COMPLIMENTARY PEANUTS!

HOW DID THE *BOOK* INSULT THE *MAGAZINE?*

... SHE CALLED HIM *SPINELESS!*

ON WHICH *CD* DO YOU FIND THE *ALPHABET SONG?*

... ON THE *ABCD!*

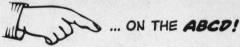

WHAT DO *MOVIE-STAR MONSTERS* SAY?

... *"BOO-RAY FOR HOLLYWOOD!"*

A PIG
+ A CENTIPEDE
―――――――――
BACON AND LEGS

WHAT DOES A *LAWYER* WEAR TO *COURT?*

... *A LAW SUIT!*

WHAT DOES A *GARDENER* DO
WHEN SHE QUITS *WEEDING?*

... SHE THROWS IN THE *TROWEL!*

WHY DID THE
LADDER FAIL
HIS *TEST?*

... HE HAD
ALL THE *RUNG*
ANSWERS!

WHY WAS THE *RUNNER*
AT *THIRD BASE* SO *SAD?*

... BECAUSE THERE'S NO PLACE LIKE *HOME!*

A JOKE WRITER
+ A PICKLE
———————————
A RID-DILL

Oh, no... it's **The Moe & Joe Show!** ® *Moe*: Say, Joe! What does the elephant use to build up his muscles?

Joe: Well, Moe...: a Dumbo-bell!

WHAT'S *RED, WHITE,* AND *BLUE* AND TASTES *SWEET?*

... YANKEE DOODLE *CANDY!*

WHEN DO *YOU* WEAR A *WATCH* ON YOUR *FINGER?*

... WHEN IT'S *DIGIT*-AL!

WHERE DID THE *BABY BAND* PLAY THEIR *FIRST CONCERT?*

... *LITTLE ROCK!*

W HY DID **DONNER** AND **BLITZEN** LET **RUDOLPH** LEAD THE **REINDEER** TEAM?

... THEY DIDN'T WANT TO **PASS** THE **BUCK!**

A CAR
+ A BABY BEAR
―――――――――
TAXI CUB

WHAT KIND OF *DRIVER* NEVER *GETS ANYWHERE?*

... A *SCREWDRIVER!*

WHAT KIND OF *FLOWER* DID THE *ROPE* SEND TO THE *STRING?*

... *FORGET-ME-KNOTS!*

WHEN THE *DISH* RAN AWAY WITH THE *SPOON,* WHERE DID THEY GO?

... *CHINA!*

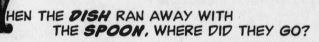

Oh, no... it's **The Moe & Joe Show!** ® *Moe*: Say, Joe! What takes six weeks at the nail salon?

 Joe: Well, Moe... a centipede getting her nails done!

WHAT DO **YOU** CALL A **TELEPHONE** PLACED NEXT TO A **WINDOW?**

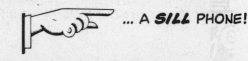 ... A **SILL** PHONE!

HAT DID THE **HAMBURGER** SAY TO THE **BOTTLE** WHILE RUNNING DOWN THE **STREET?**

... "**CATCH UP!**"

WHAT KIND OF *TELEGRAM* DO YOU GET FROM A *PARALLEL UNIVERSE?*

... A *PARALLEL*-A-GRAM!

WHAT *BARKS* LIKE A *DOG?*

... *A DOG!*

MEOW!

WHAT KIND OF *SOUP* WEIGHS *1000 POUNDS?*

... *ONE TON* SOUP!

@ MAD ADD JOKE!

BUGS BUNNY
+ PLACE TO SLEEP
―――――――――
BED BUGS

WHERE DOES A **COWBOY** BORROW **MONEY?**

... FROM THE **LOAN ARRANGER!**

HOW DID THE **TOUPEE**
GET STARTED
IN THE **MOVIES?**

... HE GOT A
SMALL PART!

$$\frac{\text{A PURPLE DINOSAUR} + \text{AN EARTHQUAKE}}{\text{BARNEY RUBBLE}}$$

Oh, no... it's **The Moe & Joe Show!** ® *Moe*: Say, Joe! Who did the bee call when he was hungry?

Joe: Well, Moe... a call-iflower!

WHAT KIND OF *WIZARD* MAKES *PASTA?*

... A *SAUCE*-EROR!

HOW DO *RAPPERS* GREET EACH OTHER IN *SWITZERLAND?*

... THEY *YO*-DEL!

WHY DID THE *KID* IN *MUSIC CLASS* GET SENT TO THE *PRINCIPAL'S OFFICE?*

 ... HE WAS A *TREBLE* MAKER!

I SCREAM U SCREAM!

DEPARTMENT

WHAT'S A *SNAKE'S* FAVORITE *ICE CREAM?*

... *ASP*-BERRY!

HAT'S A *MONSTER'S* FAVORITE *ICE CREAM?*

... *SHOCK*-OLATE!

WHAT'S AN *ACTOR'S* FAVORITE *ICE CREAM?*

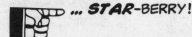 ... *STAR*-BERRY!

HAT'S AN *EGOMANIAC'S* FAVORITE *ICE CREAM?*

... *VAIN*-ILLA!

JELLYFISH
+ HUMAN BEINGS
———————————
JELLY-BEANS

WHY DID THE **POLICE DOG**
SAY **"QUACK QUACK"**?

... HE WAS **UNDERCOVER!**

WHAT DID THE **BOY** SAY TO HIS **BROTHER**
AT THE **PET STORE?**

... **"THAT'S YOUR** BIRD; THIS IS **MYNA!"**

HOW DO *YOU* GET *CHOCOLATE MILK?*

... YOU *MILK CHOCOLATES!*

WHAT'S *BLACK* AND *WHITE* AND *SHOWS OFF?*

... FROSTY THE *SHOW*-MAN!

WHAT DID THE *REFLECTION* SAY TO THE *DOCTOR?*

... "I DON'T *FEEL* LIKE *MYSELF!*"

 @ **MAD ADD** JOKE!

A FISH + COMPUTER MESSAGES

EEL-MAIL

WHY WAS THE *WEATHERMAN* SO *SCARED?*

... BECAUSE HE WAS TERRIFIED OF *FAHRENHEIGHTS!*

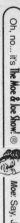

WHERE DID THE *ZOO KEEPER* SIGN HIS *NEW CONTRACT?*

 ... ON THE *DOTTED LION!*

HAT DOES A *GHOST* SAY WHEN HE MAKES A *MISTAKE?*

... "I MADE A *BOO-BOO!*"

WHICH *COUNTRY'S CAPITAL* IS HAVING A *POPULATION EXPLOSION?*

... IT'S *DUBLIN*, IRELAND!

WHAT'S *WHITE, ROUND, CLIMBS* THE *EMPIRE STATE BUILDING,* AND *SWATS PLANES?*

... *PING-PONG!*

HAT DO *YOU* CALL A *SNOW STORM* IN *OZ?*

... THE *BLIZZARD* OF OZ!

WHAT IS A **RABBIT'S** FAVORITE **JEWELRY**?

... ANYTHING MADE OF **14 CARROT GOLD!**

A COW
+ KERMIT
———————
MOO-PETS

WHERE DOES *HUMPTY DUMPTY* LIKE TO *SHOP?*

... AT *WALL*-MART!

WHO WEARS *TIGHTS* AND *SWINGS* FROM THE *CURTAINS?*

... THE *DRAPED CRUSADER!*

@ MAD ADD JOKE!

$$\frac{\text{PICASSO} + \text{CUTTING THE CHEESE}}{\text{A FARTIST}}$$

WHAT DO *YOU* CALL A *DINOSAUR* FROM *TEXAS?*

... TYRANNOSAURUS *TEX!*

W HAT DID THE *SLEEPY KING* SAY TO THE *BRAVE DRAGON SLAYER?*

... *"GOOD KNIGHT!"*

WHERE DID THEY PUT THE *BURGER* WHEN HE WAS *ARRESTED?*

... IN THE *PATTY WAGON!*

Oh, no... it's **The Moe & Joe Show!** ® *Moe*: Say, Joe! Why are aardvarks bad neighbors?

 Joe: Well, Moe... they're so nose-y!

HOW DO *YOU* KEEP *FLIES* OUT OF THE *YARD?*

... HIRE AN *OUTFIELDER!*

Why is a *BASEBALL GAME* LIKE A *PANCAKE?*

... ITS SUCCESS DEPENDS ON THE *BATTER!*

WHAT DID THE *POLICEMAN* SAY TO THE *NOISY MOTORIST?*

... "*LOOK BEFORE YOU BEEP!*"

WHAT *MESSAGE* DID THE *BAT* HEAR ON THE *PHONE?*

... "PLEASE *HANG UP-SIDE DOWN* AND TRY AGAIN!"

WHY WAS THE *PIG* THROWN OUT OF THE *FOOTBALL GAME?*

... HE PLAYED *DIRTY!*

HO INVENTED AN *AIRPLANE* THAT *COULDN'T FLY?*

... THE *WRONG BROTHERS!*

HOW DO **YOU** FEEL WHEN YOU
VISIT **NIAGARA FALLS?**

... YOU'LL NEVER **GET OVER IT!**

IF **APRIL SHOWERS** BRING **MAY FLOWERS,**
WHAT DO **MAY FLOWERS** BRING?

... **PILGRIMS!**

WHAT DO **YOU** CALL A **TRAIN** THAT PUTS
MONEY UNDER YOUR **PILLOW?**

... THE **TOOT**-FAIRY!

ITALY
+ A REFEREE
——————————
ROMAN UMPIRE

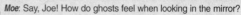

Oh, no... it's **The Moe & Joe Show!** ® *Moe*: Say, Joe! How do ghosts feel when looking in the mirror?

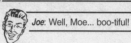

Joe: Well, Moe... boo-tiful!

HAT DO *SKATERS* USE TO *SHAVE* WITH?

... A *ROLLER-BLADE!*

WHAT DOES A *BLACK, ORANGE,* AND *WHITE CAT* USE IN *MATH CLASS?*

... A *CALICO*-LATER!

WHAT KIND OF *BOOKS* DOES A *RACECAR DRIVER* LIKE TO *READ?*

... *AUTO*-BIOGRAPHIES!

WHAT *FISH* GOES BEST WITH *PEANUT BUTTER?*

... *JELLY FISH,* OF COURSE!

WHEN DOES A *HOUSE* KNOW THAT SOMETHING IS *WRONG?*

 ... WHEN IT GETS A LOT OF *STAIRS!*

@ **MAD ADD JOKE!**

T-REX
+ OUCH
―――――――
DINO-SORE

ON WHAT DOES A **RAPPER** WRITE HIS **LYRICS?**
... **RAPPING PAPER,** OF COURSE!

WHY DO **HECKLE** AND **JECKLE** STICK **TOGETHER?**

... THEY'RE VEL-**CROWS!**

HOW DOES **LETTUCE** GET **AROUND TOWN?**

... IT TAKES A **HORSE-DRAWN CABBAGE!**

WHAT'S A **POLYGON?**

... A **PARROT** THAT ESCAPED FROM ITS **CAGE!**

$$\frac{\text{YANKEE STADIUM} + \text{MISS PIGGY}}{\text{BALL PORK}}$$

WHAT DO **YOU** CALL A **BOOMERANG'S KID?**

 ... A **BABY BOOMER**-ANG!

WHAT *FARM ANIMAL* GETS A *SORE THROAT* MORE THAN ANY OTHER?

... A *HOARSE!*

WHAT *STATE* IS *HUMPTY DUMPTY* FROM?

... *YOLK*-LAHOMA!

EDUCATOR
+ GOLF
─────────
TEACHER'S PUTT

WHAT'S A *RAPPER'S* FAVORITE *KINDERGARTEN ACTIVITY?*

... *RAP*-TIME!

HOW COULD *YOU* TELL THAT THE *RAPPER* WAS IN *LOVE?*

... HE WAS EN-*RAP*-TURED!

OW DO *YOU* GET *DOWN* FROM A *MULE?*

... YOU DON'T GET DOWN FROM A MULE, YOU GET *DOWN* FROM A *GOOSE!*

Oh, no... it's **The Moe & Joe Show!** ® *Moe*: Say, Joe! What's the best time to have a midnight snack?

 Joe: Well, Moe... duh! Midnight!

WHAT HAPPENED WHEN **FRANKENSTEIN** DRANK A **GLASS** OF **MILK?**

... HE MADE THE **MILK SHAKE!**

HOW DID THE **SNAKE** KEEP HIS **WINDSHIELD** CLEAN?

... WITH A WINDSHIELD **VIPER!**

WHAT DID **ONE SHOE** SAY TO
THE OTHER **SHOE?**

... "YOUR **LACE** IS FAMILIAR!"

WHY DID
THE **CORNSTALK**
GO TO THE **MALL?**

... TO GET
ITS **EAR**
PIERCED!

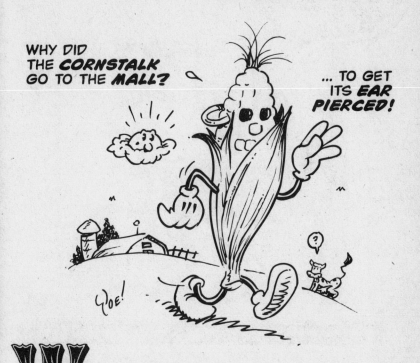

WHEN DO **DUCKS** HAVE **SIX LEGS?**

... WHEN THEY'RE **HUEY, LOUIE,** AND **DEWEY!**

KING OF THE APES
+ UNCLE SAM
—————————————
TARZAN STRIPES

Oh, no... it's **The Moe & Joe Show!** ® **Moe:** Say, Joe! What did one cow say when the other one farted?

Joe: Well, Moe... "I herd that!"

WHAT DID THE *RED ROSE* SAY TO THE *PINK ROSE?*

... "WHAT'S UP, *BUD!*"

 HAT *BODY OF WATER* DO YOU FIND BETWEEN THE *ATLANTIC* AND *PACIFIC OCEANS?*

... TENNES-*SEA!*

WHAT'S A *WITTLE BABY'S DINNER* CALLED?

 ... A WINNER!

WHAT DO *FROGS* SPREAD ON THEIR *TOAST?*

... BUTTER-*FLIES!*

WHAT DO *YOU* CALL A *REALLY COOL FROG?*

... *TOAD*-ALLY AWESOME!

WHAT DO *YOU* GET WHEN YOU CROSS A *FOOTBALL PLAYER* WITH A *MUPPET?*

... *TACKLE-ME-ELMO!*

Oh, no... it's **The Moe & Joe Show!** ® *Moe*: Say, Joe! Where were you when the lights went out?

 Joe: Well, Moe... in the dark!

WHAT DO *YOU* CALL A *CRAZY SPACEMAN?*

... AN ASTRO-*NUT!*

WHAT DO *YOU* CALL A GROUP OF *ALIENS* THAT *PLAY INSTRUMENTS* AND *WALK* IN *PARADES?*

... A *MARTIAN* BAND!

@ MAD ADD JOKE!

BUGS BUNNY
+ KERMIT THE FROG
―――――――――――――
BUNNY RIBBIT!

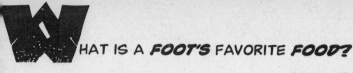 HAT IS A *FOOT'S* FAVORITE *FOOD?*

... POTA-*TOES!*

WHY DID THE *BROOM* TAKE A *NAP?*

... BECAUSE IT WAS *SWEEP*-Y!

WHAT DID THE *SALADS* SAY AFTER *GETTING STUCK* IN THE *REFRIGERATOR?*

... "*LETTUCE* OUT!"

Oh, no... it's **The Moe & Joe Show!** ® *Moe*: Say, Joe! Why was the cocoa never on time?

 Joe: Well, Moe... because it was choco-late!

WHY DID THE ***TURKEY*** PLAY ***DRUMS*** IN THE BAND?

... BECAUSE HE HAD THE ***DRUMSTICKS!***

HERE IS ***ONE PLACE*** YOU'LL NEVER FIND A ***DOG?***

... A ***FLEA***-MARKET!

WHAT DID THE ***HAND*** DO AFTER IT ***GRADUATED*** FROM ***HIGH SCHOOL?***

... IT JOINED THE ***ARM***-Y!

HOW DOES THE *MOTHER CLOWN* GET THE *BABY CLOWN* OUT OF *BED?*

... SHE YELLS *"WACKY* UP!"

HAT DID THE *TEACHER* SAY TO THE *KITTEN* WHEN IT WAS LEARNING TO *SPEAK?*

... "PRACTICE MAKES *PURR*-FECT!"

@ **MAD ADD JOKE!**

$$\frac{MONEY + PERFUME}{DOLLARS \ \& \ SCENTS}$$

WHAT IS A **TRUCK DRIVER'S** FAVORITE **FOOD?**

... **MACK**-ARONI AND CHEESE!

WHERE DID THE **KING** GO TO **COLLEGE?**

... **PRINCE**-TON!

WHERE DOES **SANTA** KEEP ALL OF HIS **RED SUITS?**

... IN THE **CLAUS**-ET!

WHAT DID THE **GUITAR** SAY TO THE **GUITAR PLAYER?**

... "STOP **PICKING** ON ME!"

WHAT DO **RABBITS** USE TO **STYLE** THEIR **FUR?**

... **HARE** SPRAY!

Oh, no... it's *The Moe & Joe Show!* ®

Moe: Say, Joe! Why did the cows get married?

Joe: Well, Moe... because they loved each udder!

WHAT DID ONE *TELEPHONE* GIVE THE OTHER FOR *VALENTINE'S DAY?*

... A *RING!*

WHAT ARE THE *COOLEST* PARTS OF A *SALAD?*

... THE *RAD*-ISHES!

WHAT DO *FROGS* USE TO *COOK?*

... *FLY*-ING PANS!

**HAT DO *YOU* CALL IT WHEN A *MARTIAL ARTS EXPERT* GETS *SICK*?**

... KUNG *FLU*!

WHAT DO *YOU* CALL A *DUCK* THAT *TURNS* INTO A *VAMPIRE*?

... *QUACK*-ULA!

WHAT *FRUIT* CAN *YOU* DRINK *SODA THROUGH*?

 ... A *STRAW*-BERRY!

 JOKE!

A PIG
+ AN EVERGREEN
―――――――――
PORKY-PINE

Oh, no... it's **The Moe & Joe Show!** ® **Moe**: Say, Joe! What's the best day to go to the beach?

Joe: Well, Moe... Sun-day!

WHAT *TIME* DO *CHICKENS* GO TO *SLEEP?*

... AROUND 9 O'*CLUCK!*

HOW DID THE *DETECTIVE* FIND THE *STOLEN CHRISTMAS TREE?*

... HE LOOKED FOR SANTA *CLUES!*

 WHAT DID THE *MOTHER TRAIN* SAY TO THE *BABY TRAIN* WHEN HE WAS EATING TOO *QUICKLY?*

... "*CHEW, CHEW!*"

WHY DID **MICKEY MOUSE** QUIT HIS **JOB?**

... HE WAS TIRED OF THE **RAT RACE!**

WHAT DO **YOU** CALL A **BIG GREEN MONSTER** THAT **DROOLS A LOT?**

... FRANKEN-**SLIME!**

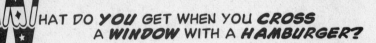

HAT DO **YOU** GET WHEN YOU **CROSS** A **WINDOW** WITH A **HAMBURGER?**

... WINDSHIELD **WHOPPERS!**

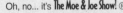
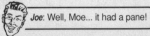

WHAT DID THE **ARTIST** SAY AT THE **START** OF THE **DUEL?**

... "**DRAW!**"

W HAT **DAY** OF THE **WEEK** DO **CHICKENS** HATE?

... **FRY**-DAY!

a **MAD ADD** JOKE!

$$\frac{LAWYER + FROG'S\ HOUSE}{LEGAL\ PAD}$$

WHAT DO **PENGUIN CONSTRUCTION WORKERS** USE TO **BLOCK TRAFFIC?**

... **SNOW** CONES!

HOW DID THE *HORSE* GREET HIS *NEXT DOOR FRIEND?*

... "GOOD MORNING, *NEIGH*-BOR!"

FACELIFT
+ FISH
_____
PLASTIC STURGEON

WHAT DO **YOU** GET WHEN YOU **CROSS** A **GREYHOUND** WITH **FRENCH FRIES?**

... **FAST FOOD!**

WHAT **GIRL** IS BETWEEN **12** AND **20** **YEARS OLD?**

... CHRIS-**TEEN!**

WHAT DO **YOU** CALL A **GIANT FISH** THAT **CLIMBS** THE **EMPIRE STATE BUILDING?**

... KING **COD!**

 Oh, no... it's **The Moe & Joe Show!** ® *Moe*: Say, Joe! What boy has a pocket full of change?

 Joe: Well, Moe... Nickel-as!

WHAT DO *YOU* CALL A *VEGETABLE* THAT'S *OLD* AND *ROTTEN?*

... ASPARA-*GROSS!*

HEN DO *ICE CREAM* AND *HOT FUDGE* LIKE TO *GET TOGETHER?*

... ON *SUNDAE*-S!

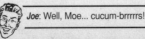

You Have

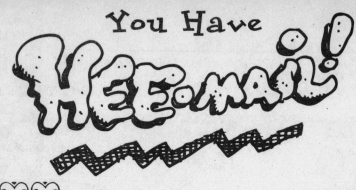

HEE-mail!

OW DO **HORNETS** SEND **COMPUTER MESSAGES?**

... THROUGH **BEE**-MAIL!

OW DOES **AQUAMAN** SEND **COMPUTER MESSAGES?**

... THROUGH **EEL**-MAIL!

OW DO **BOYS** SEND **COMPUTER MESSAGES?**

... THROUGH **HE**-MAIL!

OW DO **CHEAPSKATES** SEND **COMPUTER MESSAGES?**

... THROUGH **FREE**-MAIL!

HOW DO *GIRLS* SEND
COMPUTER MESSAGES?

... THROUGH *FE*-MAIL!

HOW DO *YOU* SEND *COMPUTER MESSAGES* TO *YOURSELF?*

... USE *ME*-MAIL!

HOW DO *SNOW LOVERS* SEND
COMPUTER MESSAGES?

... THROUGH *SKI*-MAIL!

HOW DO THE *IRISH* SEND
COMPUTER MESSAGES?

... THROUGH *BLARNEY*-MAIL!

HOW DOES A *BAKER* SEND
COMPUTER MESSAGES?

... THROUGH *COOKIE*-MAIL!

HOW DO THE *ENGLISH* SEND
COMPUTER MESSAGES?

... THROUGH *TEA*-MAIL!

HOW DO THE *FRENCH* SEND
COMPUTER MESSAGES?

... THROUGH *OUI*-MAIL!

WHAT DO *YOU* CALL A *BABY STABLE?*

... A NEW-*BARN!*

WHY WAS THE *LIVING ROOM* ARRESTED?

... BECAUSE IT WAS IN POSSESSION OF AN *ARMED CHAIR!*

@ MAD ADD JOKE!

$$\frac{\text{DOG + FOOTBALL PLAYER}}{\text{GOLDEN RECEIVER}}$$

WHY DID **ROSEMARY** TAKE A **SHORTCUT?**

... TO SAVE **THYME!**

WHAT HAPPENED WHEN THE **TWO BAKERS** MET?

... IT WAS **LOAF** AT FIRST SIGHT!

HAT DO **YOU** CALL A **REPTILE** THAT DOESN'T LIKE TO TAKE THE **STAIRS?**

... AN ALLI-**VATOR!**

WHAT DO **HUNTERS** USE TO **STYLE** THEIR **HAIR?**

... **MOOSE!**

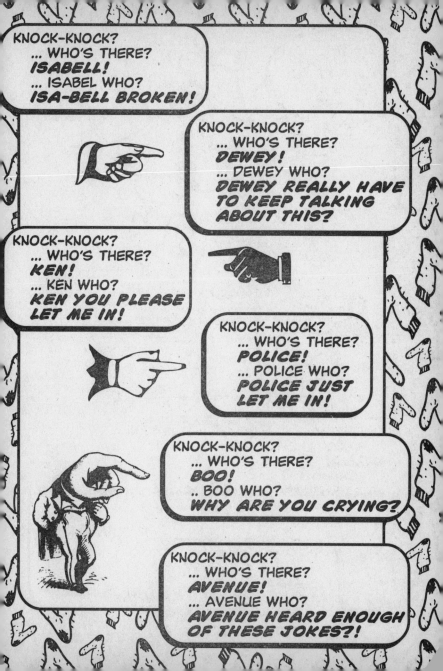

WHAT **FANCY ANIMAL** IS ALSO A **FLOWER?**

 ... A **DANDY LION!**

HAT **PERSON** LIKES **CAMPING** MORE THAN ANYONE?

... THE PRESI-**TENT!**

WHAT **PART** OF A **TELEVISION** IS MOST LIKE A **WINDOW?**

... THE **SCREEN!**

HAT DOES A **GENIE** USE TO **BLOW** HIS **NOSE?**

... **WISH**-UES!

 **BEES + BIRDS**
―――――――――
KILLER BEAKS!

HOW DO *SINGLE CATS* MEET *EACH OTHER?*

... IN THE *PURR*-SONALS!

WHAT IS *MONEY* PRINTED ON?

... *PAY*-PER!

WHAT'S THE *LOUDEST BOOK* IN YOUR *HOUSE?*

 ... THE *YELL*-OW PAGES!

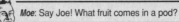

WHAT HAPPENED WHEN THE *NOSE* WROTE HIS *AUTOBIOGRAPHY?*

... IT BECAME A BEST-*SMELLER!*

WHAT IS A *VAMPIRE'S* FAVORITE *FOOD?*

... *NECK*-TARINES!

WHAT DOES A *GHOST* USUALLY ORDER IN A
RESTAURANT?

... FILET OF *SOUL!*

WHAT **FRUITS** ARE HIRED TO WORK
ON A **SHIP?**

... **NAVAL** ORANGES!

WHY DID
THE **WAITRESS**
QUIT HER
JOB?

... SHE
COULD **DISH**
IT OUT BUT
SHE COULDN'T
TAKE IT!

HY DIDN'T THE **TURKEY** EAT ANYTHING
ON **THANKSGIVING?**

... BECAUSE IT WAS **STUFFED!**

Oh, no... it's **The Moe & Joe Show!** ® *Moe*: Say, Joe! What pet sleeps on the porch?

 Joe: Well, Moe... a door mutt!

A PIMPLE
+ CAR ACCIDENT

RASH TEST DUMMIES!

WHAT *DIRECTS* CARS IN *CHOCOLATE TOWN?*

... TRUFFLE LIGHTS!

**W**HAT *HAPPENED* TO THE *DOG* WHO *ROBBED* A *BANK?*

... HE GOT *COLLARED!*

WHY DID THE *BUSINESSMAN* FALL *ASLEEP* AT *WORK?*

... BECAUSE HE WAS THE CHAIRMAN OF THE *BORED!*

WHAT DOES A *SPORTS FAN* CARVE ON *HALLOWEEN?*

... A *JOCK*-O'-LANTERN!

Oh, no... it's **The Moe & Joe Show!** ® *Moe:* Say, Joe! Why is pizza dough so in demand?

 Joe: Well, Moe... because people knead it!

WHAT DOES **KEN** SAY WHEN HE SEES **BARBIE?**

... "HELLO, **DOLLY!"**

WHAT **SHIP-WORKER** ALWAYS **WEARS** A **HAT?**

... THE **CAP**-TAIN!

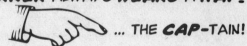

HAT DO **YOU** USE TO **GET INTO** A **HAUNTED HOUSE?**

... A **SKELETON** KEY!

Oh, no... it's **The Moe & Joe Show!** ® *Moe*: Say, Joe! What do farm animals lounge around on?

 Joe: Well, Moe... a cow-ch!

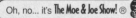